The Daughter's Curse

Poems

Jennifer Givhan

THE DAUGHTER'S CURSE
Jennifer Givhan

All Poems © 2017 Jennifer Givhan

First Edition
April 2018

ISBN 978-1-387-70740-9

Yellow Flag Press
yellowflagpress.com

YFP-144

Contents

The Daughter's Curse

When I was a girl

something terrible

Warn the Young Ones

First war   She polishes the spine of her own
flesh   Tethered nerve   strangling cord   She

burial mounds   She rituals   She
corn stalks in rustling fields   Nothing tribe

nothing sex   Rock for riverbed   Notched
with flint   Second war   She needs less   Sequoia

burns   Cities   In her body   wrappings
of bodies   She debates running   She debates peeling

skin   She stops debating   begins praying without
knees   Not *for* rain   *Prays* rain   Holy nothing

unlaces nothing remembered nothing
forgiven—   Come others   Third war

She is a void in the particle machine   She is dust
Fourth war she loses the need for water   She loses

all taste   Rain brings each earthwormed corpse   Nothing
ugly   Turn not   Her face from the dead   She

resurgence   She fable of bee boxes
& honey   She ark of some lost territory

of animals   She zebras   She aardvarks
She dredges the flooded streets of her   She gutters

Fifth war   She grows stronger   All that can be
taken she takes   All that can be eaten

she swallows   All that can be broken she
pulls into her belly & releases   Nothing is whole

Sixth war   She loses her appetite   Her bones brittle
The cabbage in the broth bitters   She

pulls from ribcages   Hearts   Uses them
as weapons   Seventh war   The cord she began with

Nothing like a noose   She would rest   Longs for nothing
but rest   Each threaded backbone slips its knot   Nothing

transforms   She wants to tell you this is the end   She wants—

When the Jornada del Muerto* had a windpipe

& she was choking on deviled eggs
    with yellow mustard & paprika sprinkles
at her mama's book club picnic in the backyard

where she used to play rag dolls alone
    until she found her ghost sister
Nieve white as snowcone before the juice

if she longed for more than salt flats
    or sand dunes or lava flows beyond the fence's
thick irrigation pipes   if she was clutching

her scarf & flailing while the mamas
    read on   pages thick with ink the color
of the crows in her dark eyes   if she was lost

& lonely but none of that mattered
    now she was turning blue with swallowing
spongy egg pieces down the wrong tube—

I would wrap my red arms around her
    & python-squeeze until she spit them out
Maybe her mama stopped hugging her

when her father left   Maybe her mama cannot see
    her baby white sister   lightly
snowing on the desert cacti   corseting

cane cholla like a muted holiday wasteland
    Maybe her mama didn't even notice
she too had almost gone away

on the xeriscaping   not breathing nothing—
    not grownup conversations or party cups
of pink iced lemonade or stifling

winter air   Let the desert choke
    Let her have something inside
that nearly strangles her to tell

Then   if she needed me to   I would reach
    inside & scrape the ridges of her burning
throat until the lump stopped growing…

If she needed me to   I would lash myself
    to her basalt neck   make myself a scar

* *The Jornada del Muerto (Spanish for "single day's journey of the dead one") is a desert in Southern New Mexico*

Nieve in the Desert Circus

Again my ghosted sister parades herself
before sunset   glistening & sharp-toothed as
cacti rungs crackling from the red rocks
dividing the landscape into just three rings   Southwestern
elephants are shaped like bison   their white-horned skulls
framing the first act   reviving the wild dead who've
gone ahead   she's gotten so good at it—Nieve
hair like snow   Nieve tightroping white dunes of sand
I round up the afternoon's contestants   a vulture-picked
jackalope we can tell was regal once   his crown of antlers still
knotting his temples   a scorpion mouse   our miniature
lion   night howl we're certain will return   the lunatic-
mama who left us to this madness   our perpetual
necropsy in this unenchanted land where we can
only pretend   But oh   we've gotten so good at it—
performing in the center ring   two girls
quicksilver as the desert herself   where survival means
running toward the nearest cave   where
survival means imagination like water   means
tracing ourselves in the petroglyphs   chiseling our stories
under the ancients'   In the final ring   where nightfall
veins the big-top sky with starlight   hope
wears a gown of fire   turning fortune-teller   she shows us
x-ray sharp   how this spectacle will end   Nieve
yellows into morning   she melts back into dreams   not
zombie sister   no   The real & saving thing

The Dying Girl & the Date Palm

Come find me under the black persimmon tree   Mama
where prayers bear wrinkled fruit   bear messages home

come tend me at sunrise   like sweeping
a grave   offering fresh tortillas

rolled each morning   menudo steaming on the stove
My patch of yellowing in the grass   my lungs culling holes

in the sweet so close to my palms I can nearly grasp
What does a mouth hold but secrets   What tongue in mine

What bone-handled crotch & tissue paper wadded to staunch
the bleeding   The boy on the bicycle called my name   pulled

it from my mouth like meat from the seed &
his older brother with a truck   A hole in the floorboard

A hole in the world
                    Persimmons call themselves stories

of the gods   Mama   did you also wake into the mythical
I mean   rise yourself   hold the cast of yourself

bones splitting as moonstones   as midnight   undone
Leaves fall across my eyes   Mama   come find me before I bloom

Risen Again

Anything can be a time machine
For us it was the elms grown crooked
into each other   knobby-rooted
& shooting nine-stories into the sky
I named one Risen Again
for how it branched down into dirt
then up again   snakelike   hiding places
for me & the others   But it transported only me—
& Nieve   We could disappear
into its corkscrewed trunk & be two
places at once for I'd found a way to split
myself   What the grownups didn't know
enough to dredge the river
cemetery where we'd play hide & seek
& never find   Enough to send us
where they no longer existed
But the boy the color of an oak casket who
guarded me in the tree's clearing so I could cross
would no more make it to adulthood
than any of us   I knew that about him
& loved him anyway   What did it feel like   splitting?
Like ice pops against summer heat
bare feet scalding asphalt & eggs dropping
on sidewalk to test a theory   We fried
ourselves like sizzling pork fat plucked
from the comal & dipped in chile

We held our whole bodies like a tree
after anyone had tried to chop it down
A time machine can be anything
can be one's own body   I used to catch rattlers
in the foothills for five bucks a snake
I'd leash each snake's neck so it couldn't strike
then pinch between gloved fingers into a bag
for the exotic animal collector next door
Splitting felt like that like that   like catching
but also getting caught   Whichever way I twisted
felt like shedding skin felt too tight
Whichever way I turned felt like out

Reinas de STEM

"Not only are Latinas recognized for being super sexy but they're also extremely smart
Here are just a few recognized in science & more"
– Shutterstock / anyaivanova / *Latintimes com*

Mama shapes masa into hypodermic needle
Mama shapes lump of clay & calls it my pudgy nose my pudgy face
Nursing bag is dangerously low of diabetes meds
Google says I must be sexy
less sugar more injection
Lydia Villa-Komaroff helped make those sugar sticks
I need when my blood is burning spun sugar
Mija look into the mirror at those lonjas
You're getting fat & no one wants a chubby princess
to be a STEM queen like Adriana Ocampo
Planetary Geologist at NASA
face that launched the Chicxulub among the Mayan ruins
& set even prehistoric beasts afire
Mama's chupacabra stainless steel & the biologist says *women are not socialized to believe*
they can earn a living much less be
a scientist—   But France Anne-Dominic Córdova at Los Alamos
of rays both X & gamma is no pageant queen
& Ellen Ochoa (Xicana tearing chokeweed breaking branches stem by stem) flew in space
Mama look at me look at me
                    I float   I fly

How to Build a Time Machine

Mama—
spread your legs & let the daughter

out   She will survive you   she will
carry your messed up genes

into a future you're unwilling
to imagine

Close your eyes & imagine
your daughter becoming the light

becoming godlike
in her indifference

                    Mama

we are a brilliant machine—

Daughter Page Ripped from the Symbol Sourcebook

I smudge henna above our bed   protect us
from the evil eye   rub it on our grassy

cow's forehead in the backyard   My ex mother-in-law
named me La Henna   as a joke

for how my name sounded in Spanish   like I was gringa
until she realized   my mama's Mexican too

but the apodo stuck   like red rice burnt in the belly

My husband steams the carpets with Fabuloso
purple cleanser Sally once bought from Dollar Store

picking me out dish towels & plastic table cloths
for my all-alone apartment   her son wouldn't leave

her house for mine   he didn't love me enough

I'm terrified my daughter will turn gourd & fennel
for a boy who'll believe she's no different

than the Maxim or Showtime-bodied targets
he calls women   will hold her head down   make her

swallow   The springtime smell of Callery Pear blooms
gorgeous white buds that make me gag

I spit on the sidewalk   La Henna dripping
bloodstone   ghost of a girl who'll shove bezoars

down a daughter's throat to keep her from pulling
worms from the stomach   Sex is not a plague

my husband tells me   spring cleaning our sheets
flipping our mattress   redbrick stains   corral-

gates dripping rust   relentless in a patch
of spines   darling girl   I'm sorry the body resigns

Daughter / Mirror

Catoptromancy : divination by a mirror or by crystal gazing

From the next room my husband asks her   *You want to wear a dirty dress*

Birthday cake in my hands
& my hands   stained blood-red   canned plums

When is a dress irredeemably dirty

A clutch of frozen pears picked late from the frostbitten tree   shock freeze
brittles the leaves   & they rattle like broken bones
as if winter will soon break everything

A blue balloon   a half-cut moon   a pink stitch across a muted sky   Dusk & my cold
hands   twinkling
Xmas lights remind me   we are drawn

to light   it is written into our genes—
—follow the light

I must imagine   Another way

The Demon

Hands at each bedpost   grasping the head
        of the bed   jerking   ripping hard
the sleeper from sleep   This is not a dream

Morning noises
        from the window   three brave rabbits
offering themselves to a hungry black snake

A child once begged the truth
        of her mama   That child understood
more than her keep   more than her share

of the household burden   a roof lifting like a lid
        on a boiling pot   a room that means
to hold us in as much as out—

A kitchen for consuming
        or being consumed

                    In this room
pure appetite mimics memory   its sinewy shadows—

The child must grow up
        She knows her mama's hands
are her own   & shaking

Birthright Disguise

I dreamt a woman with Mama's
crow-black hair & eyes

was unzipping a feathered demon suit
prickling at the neck

skin beneath the scales or gills
my own beige   plain & scarred—

(Face her   Face yourself) I could hear
her screaming   but I couldn't tell

how sticky the demon had grown

When I startled awake as often is the case
each time I'm frighteningly close

to understanding what happened those years
I cannot remember   thrown away

like the girlhood & teenage diaries
I burned when I got married   *a fresh start*

I'd said   although now I'm certain
that was a lie
          my daughter in her footy

pajamas stood at the bed's steep edge
watching me sleep   Or was she trying

to wake me   pull off the dark sleep
suit? I panicked   I jumped   Her eyes

shot owl wide
     The simpler story would end

with me   plucking from the pillows &
my hair   feathers   choking back

mouthfuls of scabs
    Instead   I had to ask her
I had to   (Baby   let me see   Open your mouth)

The Daughter's Curse

For ruining your body   the bruised
pear you become each night

beneath sheets
—selfsame animal since girlhood bloomed

thick as shaving cream on your legs   savage
as spilled sugar water on the kitchen tile

between crevices—

teeth meant for lacerating mattress-
beaten thoughts   for other

than this   Say the damn thing
       Let down

like milk   like memory from your blood   Curse
me with what you cannot give & keep giving

& I keep taking

Goldman's Fake Mother

In midsummer green & guilty heat
from my upstairs window I watch
the neighbor's power saws menacing
The children may be safe in another
neighbor's yard   cinderblocks for hedges
bug repellant for the spiders—
The psych ward of the nearest hospital
would send me home with anxiety meds
& the number of a friendly therapist
Consider the thought experiment
of Goldman's fake barn   except
like in a mad lib   for the word *barn*
substitute *mother*   Everything else
will remain the same   On a trip
(it doesn't matter where) the child's
father points out the objects he sees
that's a cow   that's a silo   that's a *barn*
The father has excellent eyesight
& little to distract him   we have no
reason to doubt his knowledge
Now suppose we discover the father
has entered a district full of papier-mâché
façades   without back walls or interiors
quite incapable of being used as *barns*—
so clever is their construction

that folks invariably mistake them for *barns*
& having just entered this district
the father has no experience of replicas
Whether the *barn* is genuine or not
can we say he *knows* the object to be a *barn*?
& you   dear reader? Could you tell
the difference? Is our poor father convinced?
I'm so tired   so tired   & the afternoon casts
ominous shadows from the skinflint trees
sapping all my resolve that the sun
& her brave yellow eye will continue
shining indefinitely   The children must be safe
must be laughing   except their mouths
form only silent little O's

In the Waiting Room of the Child Psychologist

My daughter through the door
                her voice a small squeaking thing

        like one of the two mice trapped
in the glass box   rusting at its hinges

                in our garden's collection of late-
summer rainwater

When I paid them my last evening vigil
        they were still filling themselves with the poison

        my husband left   No longer hurtling
    against the trick latch   they'd begun

their slow starvation

        We might have let them into the sage
    field   volcanos rising from stacks of houses

We could have made them our redemption
        in those rocky fields   not joke of glass & a desert sky

so clear any mammal might be tempted
                        beyond the irresponsible release

           to believe in saviors

We who must know I am not considering mice
           but mothers   but the god of all mothers

I fail with so little grace

Sighting

Last night in the backyard   your shawl
flung across the swing set   I found you

gnawing carrots from Mama's garden
with such a simple grace I believed

that moment you were a white rabbit
a sweet phantom animal come to lead

me somewhere strange   Moonlight greased
the mountain ranges surrounding us

gunmetal gray & fettering us to this home
we once shared   Nieve   sister new as snow

returned like the red rash on my neck
may I ask your blessing to stay?

Will you answer me? Surely those aren't worms
chafing your eyes   Not your shucked

remains littering Mama's soil   Slotted
between hedgerows you remind me what you mean

a glimpse into the other/world is enough
(you haven't left me   alone)

Three Wolf Spirits

      I watch them paw the air as if even the air
  were full with doomed rabbits

What creature in me longs to give in now
   & wild

        Once I faced in the bottle-
  brush in the scrub of dying

leaves a rabbit who didn't run but watched

I swear she watched until I could face her
no longer
   Maybe I should seek my fate with the dogs

I've scavenged my way to this place
   through times that love is scarce

      & sunlight scorches more than it creates
      I've faced in the bottle-

  rasp of dying
myself & believed those three familiar spirits
pawing at the air

    were here for me

Nieve & I Grow Up

In the last battle the unicorn bloodies her horn

Past the bosque marshlands I hear that she must
suffer   that her hooves are meant for loam

                              Listen   how nights
bloom jasmine from the salt bones   our ribcages

sprouting like burial plots   Her myth
unburies us   How we've flanked her with handprints—

reddest for love   She isn't girlhood-breaking
She isn't imagination-must-fail
                         When I was a child

something unbearable   In the last battle
I kept what belonged to me   what came into this world

with me   I became a woman like this—
              the blood was mine the blood
was mine the blood   Nieve rides back into memory

A Woman Might Want to Fly Away

After my salt bath after watching
the evening sky the way one watches

birds   I reached for my favorite dress   its
slimming V   when I saw that its crossed back

had grown a pair of wings   I carried it
flapping to the medicine cabinet   pulled out

tiny eyebrow scissors & began clipping
like loose threads from a hem   only thicker

& wilder   Then I slipped the dress
over my head   examined my reflection

slowly as a winter fog   lifting   I turned

The wings   Again   They were beating
madly   & soon I began to fly

My husband was working late
I called to my children   but the door

was closed or they pretended
not to hear   & I couldn't control

the dress   I tried lifting it over my head
but it was stronger & carried me

toward the balcony glass
slamming me   again & again

until I unfumbled the latch
            She felt herself much lighter

I said aloud so the dress could hear
The night fell cool   Was another woman

watching as I blended into sunset
dipping from sight   At last I grew tired

of flying   & hunger & cold
I struggled   The dress fell onto a field

I   nearly naked   beside it

A teenager on a bike lent me his phone
so I called my mother who said

she understood   It wasn't just dresses
but any clothing   *Once a woman's reached*

a certain age   I asked   No   it was
the watching   she said   handing me a wrap

Ghost Girl in the Recovery Room

She points past the empty field
        past the ringing of a church bell   She asks who rings

the church bell   I tell her   no one now

The silverware needs shining
        in the game she's making up   She tells me

she is an empty treehouse
        & I am a moon pool

but she's the architect of my scarred abdomen
        she's set for tea   It's an ordinary weekday   The sound

of bells on rocks   or rocks for bells   she says

your mother won the heaven lottery
        & had a beautiful daughter   I remember saying

something like this to her   she's soaked it in as milk to bread

& repeats the beautiful empty of my abdomen   She
        scars the moon pool

I am a church bell

I empty past the field past the ringing of play
I remember a table

    It's an ordinary weekday
    The silverware needs shining

The Last Act

was for juggling breakables like bodies
like collectibles   the child's heart   its own

small body like a hope high enough
for a trapeze artist flinging across swings

a white kite of skin & bone   the torn white t-shirt
of a girl who dangles herself from the cold bars

of a jungle gym   how upside-down flying feels
like bodies of trees with their flickers of leaves

rustling but that wasn't the sound my body made
bewildered by boys throbbing me for fun the way

a vintage circus is fun before the lion escapes
or fire rings a body that cannot keep her safe

I went to the circus & held a spider's body
but she wasn't spindly   as I thought of a spider

nor are bodies ever just skin & bones
& hardness where one expects something softer

Reverse: A Girlhood

Unbloom the night cactus   return
honey bats to their nocturne roost

empty the prickling organ pipes   refill
every mine

Bodies in motion must
for every girl with nectar in her mouth
for every daughter filled with fruit

Deworm   restrain
    Unpollinate the desert   unslake its stubborn ventricles

skull white   bone dry
girl empty

        Within the fever
Nieve holds for me one elegant equation
one simple prayer

recant the forward flow of time   unmouth

the dirge   unchant goodbye
unbury the child   unbury

the child   (the backyard
hasn't looked this safe in years) unswallow the sky   .

Break its beak   its brittle arrow
unslung   rock split

          There is a way back

Acknowledgments

Blackbird: "Warn the Young Ones"

Blue Mesa Review Poetry Prize: "If the Jornada del Muerto* had a windpipe" (2nd place
　　　winner & included in *Sundress Publications Best of the Net 2015*)

Brambled Anthology (Sugared Water & Porkbelly Press): "Rosa & Nieve Grow Up" &
　　　"Reverse A Girlhood or Rosa y Nieve Say Goodbye to the Desert Circus"

Crab Creek Review: "A Woman Might Want to Fly Away" (republished in *Fiolet &
　　　Wing Anthology of Domestic Fabulism*)

Foundry: "Ghost Girl in the Recovery Room"

Indiana Review: "The Dying Girl & the Date Palm"

Life & Legends: "Sighting"

Madison Review: "Reverse: A Girlhood"

Menacing Hedge: "The Daughter's Curse" "Birthright Disguise" "The Demon"

The Normal School: "In the Waiting Room of the Child Psychologist"

The Offing: "Risen Again"

Passages North: "Nieve in the Desert Circus" (2015 Elinor Benedict Prize finalist)

Scissors & Spackle: "Three Wolf Spirits" (nominated for a Pushcart 2016)

Sugar House Review: "The Last Act"

Tupelo Quarterly: "The Daughter Page Ripped from the Symbol Sourcebook"

About the Author

Jennifer Givhan is a Mexican-American poet from the Southwestern desert. She is the author of *Landscape with Headless Mama* (2015 Pleiades Editors' Prize), *Protection Spell* (2016 Miller Williams Series, University of Arkansas Press), and *Girl with Death Mask* (2017 Blue Light Books Prize, Indiana Review / Indiana University Press). Her chapbooks include *Lifeline* (Glass Poetry Press) and *Lieserl Contemplates Resurrection* (dancing girl press). Her honors include a National Endowment for the Arts Fellowship in Poetry, a PEN/Rosenthal Emerging Voices Fellowship, The Frost Place Latin@ Scholarship, The 2015 Lascaux Review Poetry Prize, The Pinch Poetry Prize, and her work has appeared or is forthcoming in *Best of the Net, Best New Poets, Poetry Daily, Verse Daily, AGNI, Ploughshares, Poetry, TriQuarterly, Boston Review, Crazyhorse, Blackbird,* and *The Kenyon Review*. She is Editor-in-Chief at *Tinderbox Poetry Journal,* and she lives with her family in New Mexico near the Sleeping Sister volcanoes.

Made in the USA
Columbia, SC
30 June 2019